conte

G000137933

British & North American Readers:
Please note that Australian cup and
spoon measurements are metric. A quick
conversion guide appears on page 63.
A glossary explaining unfamiliar terms
and ingredients begins on page 60.

italian
essentials

Where would we be without parmesan for our pasta, or mozzarella on our pizza? Other not so well known Italian staples are foccacia bread, the basis for hearty toasted sandwiches, polenta, a tasty substitute for potatoes and rice, and prosciutto, one of the world's finest hams.

parmesan

There are two types of Italian parmesan: Parmigiano Reggiano and Parmigiano Padano. Padano isn't aged as long as Reggiano, so more of it is available and it is generally much cheaper.
Reggiano is aged for about three years, sometimes longer, and as it ages it becomes harder in texture and develops a stronger more mature flavour, perfect for grating or shaving over pasta, soup and salads. It's always best to buy parmesan cheese in a piece and grate it when you need it. Pre-grated parmesan will have lost most of its flavour by the time you use it.

polenta

Polenta is the name given to both cornmeal and the dish made from it. Dry polenta (a coarsely ground cornmeal) is added to boiling salted water or stock and stirred (using a long-handled spoon because it splatters as it cooks) until it is thick and smooth.

Butter and parmesan are added for extra flavour. It can be eaten just as it is, or poured into a baking dish, cooled, cut into squares and grilled or fried. Polenta makes a nice change from rice and mixes well with Mediterranean flavours such as olives and sun-dried tomatoes. Serve it also with roasted meats or vegetables.

mozzarella

Mozzarella is a soft, elastic cheese, stretching into long strands when heated. It is used most often on pizzas, but it can also be sliced and included in a salad, and it makes a good toasted cheese sandwich. It was originally made from buffalo milk and you can still buy this at specialty cheese shops, but it is now mostly made from cows' milk. Bocconcini are small balls of fresh mozzarella, stored in whey. They must be eaten within a day or two of purchase. Store in the fridge in a covered container of water. Baby bocconcini are tiny balls of bocconcini, lovely when halved and tossed into a salad.

prosciutto crudo

Sometimes called Parma ham, this is a salted and air-cured ham, perfectly safe to eat raw. It is usually cut paper-thin and eaten with figs or slices of melon as a first course or part of an antipasto platter, but it can also be grilled or fried until crisp. Prosciutto 'cotto' (cooked ham) is also available at some delicatessens.

foccacia

This bread is usually made in a rectangular shape. It grills beautifully and is just the right thickness and texture for a grilled open sandwich. Cut the foccacia into a chunk, halve it, toast it lightly and pile on chopped salami, olives, sun-dried or fresh tomatoes, anchovies, sliced artichoke hearts and cheese. Grill it for a few minutes to warm it and melt the cheese, and you have the perfect lunch or snack.

4 swordfish

with olive paste

200g black olives, seeded

¹/₄ cup (50g) drained capers

¹/₃ cup fresh dill sprigs

²/₃ cup fresh flat-leaf parsley leaves

2 cloves garlic, chopped

2 tablespoons lemon juice

4 (800g) swordfish steaks

Blend or process olives, capers, dill, parsley, garlic and juice until almost a smooth paste.
Griddle-fry (or grill or barbecue) steaks until browned both sides and just cooked through. Spread fish steaks with olive paste.

On the table in 30 minutes

spaghetti
puttanesca

2 tablespoons olive oil

1 large brown onion
(200g), chopped finely

2 cloves garlic,
crushed

2 birdseye chillies,
seeded, chopped
finely

4 canned anchovies,
drained, chopped
finely

6 medium tomatoes
(1.2kg), chopped

1/2 cup (125ml)
vegetable stock

2 teaspoons sugar

100g black olives,
seeded, halved

2 tablespoons (30g)
drained capers

1/3 cup shredded fresh
basil leaves

375g spaghetti

Heat oil in large saucepan; cook onion and
garlic, stirring, until onion is soft. Add chilli,
anchovies, tomato, stock and sugar. Simmer,
uncovered, about 10 minutes or until sauce
thickens. Stir in olives, capers and basil.
Meanwhile, cook pasta in large pan of boiling
water, uncovered, until just tender; drain. Toss
hot pasta with half the sauce; top with
remaining sauce.

On the table in 30 minutes

500g fresh sardine fillets

plain flour

1 egg

2 tablespoons milk

2 cloves garlic, crushed

2 cups (140g) stale breadcrumbs

2/3 cup (50g) coarsely grated parmesan cheese

1/4 cup finely chopped fresh parsley

vegetable oil, for deep-frying

125g fettuccine

50g butter, chopped

freshly ground black pepper

tomato sauce

1 tablespoon olive oil

1 large (200g) brown onion, chopped finely

1/2 teaspoon ground cloves

2 tablespoons sugar

1 tablespoon white wine vinegar

1 cup (250ml) tomato juice

2 small (260g) tomatoes, seeded, chopped

sardines

Coat sardines in flour; shake off excess. Dip sardines into combined egg, milk and garlic, then combined crumbs, cheese and parsley. Deep-fry sardines, in batches, in hot oil, until browned all over and cooked through; drain on absorbent paper. Cover to keep warm.

Meanwhile, cook pasta in large saucepan of boiling water, uncovered, until just tender; drain. Combine pasta with butter and pepper. Serve sardines with pasta and hot Tomato Sauce.

Tomato Sauce Heat oil in small saucepan; cook onion, stirring, until soft. Add cloves; cook, stirring, until fragrant. Stir in sugar, vinegar and juice; simmer, uncovered, about 10 minutes or until sauce thickens slightly. Stir in tomato, stir until hot.

On the table in 40 minutes

8 ravioli
with burnt butter and sage

*80g piece romano
cheese*

500g fresh ravioli

80g butter

1 clove garlic, crushed

*1 tablespoon chopped
fresh sage leaves*

Using a vegetable peeler, shave cheese thinly.
Cook pasta in large saucepan of boiling water,
uncovered, until just tender; drain.
Melt butter in small saucepan; cook garlic and
sage, stirring, about 2 minutes or until butter
is browned.
Serve ravioli drizzled with butter mixture, top
with cheese.

On the table in 20 minutes

tomato and bocconcini
lamb stacks

9

2 teaspoons olive oil

*2 tablespoons
balsamic vinegar*

*2 cloves garlic,
crushed*

*16 French-trimmed
lamb cutlets*

*2 large (180g) egg
tomatoes, sliced*

*200g bocconcini
cheese, sliced*

*2 tablespoons
coarsely chopped
fresh basil leaves*

Combine oil, vinegar and garlic in small jug; brush over cutlets. Griddle-fry (or barbecue) cutlets until browned on one side; remove, place on oven tray, cooked-side up. Layer tomato, bocconcini and basil on cooked side of 8 cutlets; top with remaining 8 cutlets, cooked-side down. Tie cutlets together with kitchen string; griddle-fry (or barbecue) until browned both sides and cooked as desired.

On the table in 30 minutes

10 lamb cutlets
with pancetta and mozzarella

12 (780g) lamb cutlets

plain flour

2 eggs, beaten lightly

1 cup (70g) stale breadcrumbs

1/3 cup (25g) finely grated parmesan cheese

1 tablespoon chopped fresh basil leaves

1 tablespoon chopped fresh parsley

2 tablespoons olive oil

150g mozzarella cheese

12 slices (180g) pancetta

1 tablespoon shredded fresh basil leaves

Trim excess fat from cutlets. Using a meat mallet, pound each cutlet to flatten slightly. **Coat** cutlets in flour, shake off excess. Dip cutlets in egg, then coat in combined crumbs, parmesan and chopped herbs. Place on tray in single layer; cover, refrigerate 10 minutes.

Heat oil in large frying pan; cook cutlets, in batches, until browned both sides, drain on absorbent paper.

Cut mozzarella into twelve 5mm-thick slices. Place cutlets, pancetta and mozzarella, overlapping, in ovenproof dish. Bake, uncovered, in moderate oven about 20 minutes or until cutlets are cooked as desired. Sprinkle with basil.

On the table in 45 minutes

whitebait

with aioli

800g whitebait

plain flour

vegetable oil, for shallow-frying

lemon wedges

aioli

2 egg yolks

1 tablespoon Dijon mustard

2 tablespoons lemon juice

2 cloves garlic, crushed

3/4 cup (180ml) olive oil

1 tablespoon hot water

Toss fish in flour; shake off excess. Shallow-fry fish, in batches, in hot oil until browned and crisp; drain. Serve fish with Aioli and lemon wedges.

Aioli Blend or process egg yolks, mustard, juice and garlic until combined. Gradually add oil in thin stream while motor is operating; blend until thick. Add water while motor is operating, blend until well combined.

On the table in 25 minutes

baked
agnolotti pasta

2 x 375 packets fresh
ricotta and spinach
agnolotti

2 x 400g jars
Napoletana pasta
sauce

1 tablespoon shredded
fresh basil leaves

1 cup (100g) coarsely
grated mozzarella
cheese

$1/2$ cup (40g) finely
grated parmesan
cheese

Cook pasta in large saucepan boiling water, uncovered, until just
tender; drain.

Combine pasta, pasta sauce and basil in 2.5-litre (10-cup capacity)
ovenproof dish. Top with combined cheeses. Bake, uncovered, in
moderate oven about 15 minutes or until cheese is melted.

On the table in 30 minutes

spaghetti

with roasted vegetables

3/4 cup (180ml) olive oil

3 cloves garlic, crushed

2 medium red capsicums (400g), sliced thickly

2 medium yellow capsicums (400g), sliced thickly

1 medium kumara (400g), chopped coarsely

250g button mushrooms

200g black olives, seeded

500g spaghetti

1/2 cup finely chopped fresh flat-leaf parsley

1 tablespoon finely grated lemon rind

1/4 cup (60ml) lemon juice

100g parmesan cheese, flaked

Heat oil in small saucepan. Cool 2 minutes, add garlic; cool. Strain mixture over small jug; discard garlic.

Meanwhile, quarter capsicums, remove and discard seeds and membranes. Roast under grill or in very hot oven, skin side up, until skin blisters and blackens. Cover capsicum pieces in plastic or paper for 5 minutes; peel away skin. Slice capsicum thinly.

Combine kumara and 1 tablespoon of the cooled oil in medium baking dish; bake, uncovered, in moderate hot oven 15 minutes. Add mushrooms, olives and another tablespoon of the oil; mix well. Bake about 15 minutes or until the mushrooms are tender.

Cook pasta in large saucepan boiling water, uncovered, until just tender; drain.

Just before serving, gently toss pasta in large bowl with capsicum, kumara mixture, remaining oil, parsley, rind and juice; sprinkle with cheese.

On the table in 45 minutes

16 fettuccine
carbonara

100g piece parmesan cheese

4 baby brown onions (100g)

1 tablespoon olive oil

12 thin bacon rashers

2 cloves garlic, crushed

375g fettuccine

3 eggs, beaten lightly

3/4 cup (180ml) thickened light cream

freshly ground black pepper

Using a vegetable peeler, shave cheese thinly. Cut onions into wedges.
Heat half the oil in large frying pan; cook bacon, stirring, until crisp, drain on absorbent paper. Add remaining oil to same pan; cook onion and garlic, stirring, until onion is soft.
Cook pasta in large saucepan of boiling water, uncovered, until just tender; drain.
Return half the bacon to pan with combined eggs and cream, pasta and half the cheese. Toss gently over low heat until pasta is coated with sauce. Serve pasta topped with remaining bacon, remaining cheese and pepper.

On the table in 20 minutes

italian
baked beans

6 bacon rashers, chopped coarsely

2 large (400g) brown onions, sliced thickly

2 cloves garlic, crushed

$1/2$ cup (125ml) dry red wine

2 x 400g cans tomatoes

$1/2$ cup (125ml) water

2 x 300g cans cannellini beans, rinsed, drained

300g can red kidney beans, rinsed, drained

1 tablespoon finely chopped fresh basil leaves

1 tablespoon finely chopped fresh parsley

2 cups (140g) stale breadcrumbs

$1/4$ cup (20g) finely grated parmesan cheese

Cook bacon, onion and garlic in large heated frying pan, stirring, until bacon is browned; drain away excess fat. Add wine; cook, stirring, until wine is reduced by half. Add undrained crushed tomatoes, water and beans. Bring to boil; stir in basil and parsley.

Transfer bean mixture to oiled 2-litre (8-cup) ovenproof dish, sprinkle with 1$1/2$ cups of the breadcrumbs; bake, uncovered, in moderate oven 20 minutes.

Remove dish from oven; gently stir half the breadcrumbs into bean mixture. Top with combined remaining breadcrumbs and cheese; bake further 20 minutes or until brown and crunchy.

On the table in 50 minutes

18 baked spinach, cheese and eggplant

3 medium eggplants (1kg)

coarse cooking salt

vegetable oil, for shallow-frying

1 large brown onion (200g), chopped finely

1 clove garlic, crushed

3 medium tomatoes (600g), chopped coarsely

400g can tomatoes

1/2 cup finely chopped fresh oregano

2 teaspoons sugar

500g spinach, trimmed

250g ricotta cheese

1 egg, beaten lightly

1/2 teaspoon ground nutmeg

1 clove garlic, crushed, extra

1/2 cup (60g) coarsely grated cheddar cheese

cheese sauce

50g butter

2 tablespoons plain flour

1 1/2 cups (375ml) milk

1 cup (125g) coarsely grated cheddar cheese

Cut eggplant into 1cm slices; place on wire rack, sprinkle with salt. Stand 10 minutes. Rinse slices under cold water; drain on absorbent paper.

Heat oil in large frying pan; shallow-fry eggplant slices, in batches, until browned lightly both sides. Drain eggplant on absorbent paper.

Drain away excess oil from pan; cook onion and garlic, stirring, until onion is soft. Add fresh tomato; cook, stirring, until tomatoes are soft. Add undrained crushed tomatoes, oregano and sugar; simmer, uncovered, until mixture is reduced by half.

Meanwhile, boil, steam or microwave spinach until just wilted; drain. Squeeze excess liquid from spinach; then chop coarsely. Combine spinach, ricotta, egg, nutmeg and extra garlic in large bowl; mix well.

Spread one-third of the eggplant over base of oiled 3.5-litre (14-cup) ovenproof dish; top with tomato mixture, another one-third of the eggplant then spinach mixture. Top with the remaining eggplant and Cheese Sauce; sprinkle with cheese. Bake mixture, uncovered, in moderately hot oven about 30 minutes or until browned lightly.

Cheese Sauce Melt butter in small saucepan. Add flour; cook, stirring, until mixture thickens and bubbles. Gradually stir in milk; stir until sauce boils and thickens. Remove from heat; stir in cheese.

On the table in 50 minutes

20 lemon and artichoke rack of lamb

1 tablespoon olive oil

2 racks of lamb with 8 cutlets each

2 medium brown onions
(300g), sliced

1 medium lemon (140g)

400g can artichoke hearts, drained,
quartered

2 tablespoons (30g) drained capers

30g butter

1 teaspoon brown sugar

Heat oil in large heavy-based
baking dish, add lamb and onion,
cook until browned all over and
onion is soft. Cut lemon into
8 wedges. Add lemon and
remaining ingredients to dish;
bake, uncovered, in moderate
oven about 40 minutes or until
lamb is cooked as desired.

On the table in 50 minutes

pesto
chicken pasta

2 tablespoons olive oil

600g single chicken breast fillets, sliced

2 cloves garlic, crushed

190g jar basil pesto

500g angel hair pasta

1/2 cup (40g) finely grated parmesan cheese

Heat half the oil in large frying pan; cook chicken, in batches, until browned and cooked through. Cook garlic in same pan, stirring, until fragrant. Return chicken to pan with pesto. **Meanwhile,** cook pasta in large pan of boiling water, uncovered, until just tender; drain. **Combine** pasta with chicken mixture, cheese and remaining oil in large bowl; mix gently.

On the table in 30 minutes

spaghetti primavera
with basil butter

125g butter, softened

1/4 cup chopped fresh basil leaves

1 medium leek (350g), trimmed

1 large zucchini (150g)

500g spaghetti

1 tablespoon olive oil

1 medium red onion (170g), chopped finely

2 cloves garlic, crushed

1 large red capsicum (350g), sliced thinly

1 large yellow capsicum (350g), sliced thinly

1/2 cup (80g) pine nuts, toasted

1 tablespoon torn basil leaves

Combine butter and chopped basil in small bowl. Roll into a log shape using plastic wrap as a guide. Refrigerate until firm.

Cut leek crossways into thirds; halve each piece lengthways, then cut halved pieces into thin strips. Repeat process with zucchini.

Cook pasta in large saucepan of boiling water, uncovered, until just tender; drain. Cover to keep warm.

Heat oil in large saucepan; cook onion and garlic, stirring, until onion is soft. Add capsicum; cook, stirring, until capsicum is just browned. Add leek and zucchini; cook, stirring, until leek is just soft.

Place vegetables in large bowl with pasta; gently toss to combine. Sprinkle pasta mixture with thinly sliced basil butter, pine nuts and torn basil.

On the table in 40 minutes

roast lamb and rosemary
pizza

4 bacon rashers, sliced

2 medium brown onions (300g), sliced

2 cloves garlic, crushed

2 x 335g pizza bases

1/3 cup (80ml) tomato paste

2 medium zucchini (240g), sliced

400g cold roast lamb, sliced

250g bocconcini cheese, sliced

2 tablespoons chopped fresh rosemary

Cook bacon in large heated non-stick frying pan, stirring, until crisp; drain on absorbent paper.

Cook onion and garlic in same pan, stirring, until onion is soft.

Place pizza bases on oven trays; spread both with tomato paste. Top bases with bacon, onion mixture, zucchini, lamb, cheese and rosemary.

Bake pizzas, uncovered, in very hot oven, about 15 minutes or until cheese is melted and bases are crisp.

On the table in 30 minutes

pancetta, parmesan

and spinach salad

¹/₃ cup (80ml) olive oil

300g thin slices pancetta, chopped

1 medium red onion (170g), chopped

6 slices white bread

2 cloves garlic, crushed

100g parmesan cheese

500g baby spinach leaves

1 tablespoon balsamic vinegar

Heat 1 tablespoon of the oil in large frying pan; cook pancetta and onion, in batches, stirring, until pancetta is crisp. Drain on absorbent paper.
Remove and discard crusts from bread; cut bread into 2cm pieces. Place in medium bowl with garlic and 1 tablespoon of the remaining oil; mix well to coat bread.

Heat 1 tablespoon of the remaining oil in large frying pan; cook bread, in batches, stirring, until golden brown, drain on absorbent paper.
Using a vegetable peeler, shave cheese into thin strips.

Toss pancetta mixture and croutons in large bowl with spinach and combined remaining oil and vinegar; sprinkle cheese over top.

On the table in 30 minutes

26 minestrone
with cheesy garlic bread

1 tablespoon olive oil

1 medium white onion (150g),
sliced thickly

1 medium carrot (120g),
chopped coarsely

1 medium leek (350g), sliced thickly

2 small potatoes (240g),
chopped coarsely

100g green beans, halved

2 trimmed celery sticks (150g),
chopped coarsely

2 cloves garlic, crushed

1.5 litres (6 cups) chicken stock

400g can tomatoes

2 tablespoons tomato paste

³/₄ cup (135g) macaroni

2 small zucchini (180g),
chopped coarsely

cheesy garlic bread

8 thick slices Italian-style
bread (150g)

¹/₄ cup (60ml) olive oil

2 cloves garlic, crushed

¹/₂ cup (60g) coarsely grated
cheddar cheese

Heat oil in large saucepan; cook onion, carrot, leek, potato, beans, celery
and garlic, stirring, until onion is soft. Stir in stock, undrained crushed
tomatoes and paste. Bring to boil; simmer, covered, stirring occasionally,
about 40 minutes or until vegetables are tender. Add pasta and zucchini;
boil, uncovered, about 10 minutes or until pasta is tender.
Serve minestrone with Cheesy Garlic Bread.
Cheesy Garlic Bread Brush 1 side of bread slices with combined oil and
garlic; grill or toast on both sides until browned lightly. Sprinkle with
cheese, grill until cheese melts.

On the table in 60 minutes

florentine veal
mozzarella

250g frozen spinach, thawed

1 tablespoon olive oil

8 veal leg steaks (960g)

120g mozzarella cheese, sliced

2¹/₃ cups (600ml) bottled chunky tomato pasta sauce

1 tablespoon finely shredded fresh basil leaves

Drain spinach then, using hands, squeeze excess liquid from spinach; chop roughly.

Heat oil in large heavy-based baking dish; cook veal, in batches, until browned both sides and cooked as desired. Return veal to pan in single layer; top with spinach then cheese. Pour combined sauce and basil into dish; bake, uncovered, in moderately hot oven about 10 minutes or until cheese just melts and sauce is heated through.

On the table in 35 minutes

tortellini

with creamy mushroom sauce

80g butter

10 green onions, chopped

750g flat mushrooms, sliced

¹/₂ cup (125ml) dry white wine

300ml cream

¹/₃ cup chopped fresh parsley

750g fresh tortellini

Heat butter in large frying pan; cook onion, stirring, until soft. Add mushrooms and wine; cook, stirring, 15 minutes. Stir in cream; simmer, uncovered, about 5 minutes or until sauce thickens slightly. Stir in parsley. **Meanwhile,** cook pasta in large saucepan of boiling water, uncovered, until just tender; drain. Serve sauce over pasta.

On the table in 25 minutes

30 tomato chilli pasta with
garlic crumbs

150g sliced pancetta

500g penne

1/2 cup (125ml) olive oil

2 medium brown onions (300g), sliced

2 cloves garlic, crushed

2 birdseye chillies, seeded, chopped

8 medium egg tomatoes (600g), chopped

1/3 cup shredded fresh basil leaves

500g frozen broad beans, thawed, peeled

garlic crumbs

60g butter

2 cloves garlic, crushed

2 cups (140g) stale breadcrumbs

Grill pancetta until crisp. Cook pasta in large saucepan of boiling water, uncovered, until just tender; drain.

Heat oil in large frying pan; cook onion, garlic and chilli, stirring, until onion is soft. Add tomato, basil and beans; stir until hot. Add pasta to pan; mix gently until hot. Serve topped with pancetta and Garlic Crumbs.

Garlic Crumbs Melt butter in medium frying pan; cook garlic and crumbs, stirring, until crumbs are browned and crisp.

On the table in 40 minutes

veal
scaloppine

¼ cup (60ml) olive oil

8 veal leg steaks
(960g)

1 medium brown onion
(150g), chopped

2 cloves garlic,
crushed

⅓ cup (80ml) lemon
juice

½ cup (125ml) beef
stock

60g butter

⅓ cup chopped fresh
parsley

Heat 2 tablespoons of the oil in large frying pan; cook veal, in batches, until browned both sides and cooked as desired. Remove from pan, cover to keep warm.

Heat remaining oil in same pan; cook onion and garlic, stirring, until onion is soft. Stir in juice, stock and butter; simmer, uncovered, about 5 minutes or until sauce thickens slightly; stir in parsley. Serve sauce with veal.

On the table in 20 minutes

Dry pasta takes 10-15 minutes to cook, depending on the type; fresh pasta takes 3-5 minutes. Follow packet directions, or taste frequently to make sure you don't undercook or overcook.

tortellini alfredo

500g tortellini pasta
90g butter
2/3 cup (160ml) cream
1 cup (80g) coarsely grated parmesan cheese
1 tablespoon chopped fresh parsley

Add pasta to large saucepan boiling water. Boil uncovered until just tender; drain, return to pan.
Meanwhile, place butter and cream in medium saucepan, stir over heat until butter is combined with cream. Remove from heat, stir in cheese and parsley until smooth.
Pour sauce over pasta; toss well.

On the table in 15 minutes

fettuccine with salami and sun-dried tomatoes

500g fettuccine pasta
350g hot salami, in one piece
1 tablespoon olive oil
2 cloves garlic, crushed
290g jar sun-dried tomatoes in oil
415g can tomatoes
1 tablespoon tomato paste
2 tablespoons oregano leaves

Add pasta to large saucepan boiling water. Boil, uncovered until just tender; drain.
Meanwhile, cut salami into 1cm cubes. Heat oil in large saucepan, add garlic and salami, stir over heat until salami is crisp.
Blend or process sun-dried tomatoes, including oil from jar, undrained tomatoes and paste until combined but not smooth.
Add tomato mixture and oregano to pan and stir over heat until heated through. Serve over fettuccine.

On the table in 20 minutes

tuna penne with thyme

500g penne pasta

2 x 185g cans tuna in oil

*1 medium
red onion (170g),
chopped*

250g cherry tomatoes, quartered

1 tablespoon lemon juice

1 tablespoon fresh thyme leaves

1/2 teaspoon cracked black pepper

Add pasta to large saucepan boiling water. Boil, uncovered until just tender; drain, return to pan. **Meanwhile**, combine remaining ingredients in medium bowl. Stir tuna mixture through pasta; serve topped with flaked parmesan if desired.

On the table in 20 minutes

chicken
with silverbeet

2 tablespoons olive oil

40g butter

8 chicken thigh cutlets (1.3kg)

1 medium brown onion (150g), chopped

1 medium carrot (120g), chopped

2 trimmed celery sticks (150g), chopped

1/2 cup (125ml) chicken stock

300g silverbeet, shredded coarsely

1/2 cup (125ml) cream

Heat oil and butter in large frying pan; cook chicken, in batches, until browned all over, drain on absorbent paper. Drain all but 2 tablespoons of juices from pan. Cook onion, carrot and celery in same pan, stirring, until onion is soft.

Return chicken to pan with stock; simmer, covered, about 30 minutes or until chicken is cooked through. Remove chicken from pan, cover to keep warm.

Add silverbeet to same pan; cook, stirring, until just wilted. Add cream; stir until hot. Serve chicken with silverbeet mixture.

On the table in 30 minutes

veal
pizzaiola

8 veal leg steaks
(960g)

plain flour

1 tablespoon olive oil

30g butter

3 cloves garlic,
crushed

1/2 cup (125ml) dry
white wine

1/3 cup (80ml) chicken
stock

1/2 teaspoon sugar

3/4 cup (180ml) tomato
puree

1 tablespoon chopped
fresh oregano

1 tablespoon drained
capers

3/4 cup (90g) seeded
black olives

Toss veal in flour, shake off excess. Heat oil and butter in large frying pan;
cook veal, in batches, until browned both sides, drain on absorbent paper.
Cook garlic in same pan, stirring, until browned lightly. Add wine, stock,
sugar and puree; simmer, uncovered, until thickened slightly. Add
oregano, capers, olives and veal to pan; simmer, uncovered, about
3 minutes or until veal is tender.

On the table in 25 minutes

36 veal medallions with olive paste

2 cups (100g) firmly packed fresh parsley sprigs

$1/2$ cup (60g) seeded black olives

2 tablespoons (30g) drained capers

1 tablespoon lemon juice

1 clove garlic, crushed

4 veal eye fillet medallions (800g)

8 slices prosciutto (120g)

Blend or process parsley until finely chopped. With motor operating, add olives, capers, juice and garlic; blend until almost smooth.

Spread olive mixture around edge of each medallion; wrap 2 slices prosciutto around each piece to cover olive mixture, secure with toothpicks. Griddle-fry (or grill or barbecue) veal until browned both sides and cooked as desired. Just before serving, remove toothpicks.

On the table in 40 minutes

veal

parmigiana

2 teaspoons olive oil

1 medium white onion (150g), chopped finely

2 cloves garlic, crushed

400g can tomatoes

$1/4$ cup (60ml) tomato paste

1 tablespoon balsamic vinegar

1 teaspoon sugar

1 tablespoon shredded fresh basil leaves

2 small eggplants (460g)

8 veal leg steaks (960g)

$1^1/2$ cups (150g) grated pizza cheese

Heat oil in small saucepan; cook onion and garlic, stirring, until onion is soft. Add undrained crushed tomatoes, paste, vinegar and sugar; simmer, uncovered, about 10 minutes or until sauce thickens, stir in basil.
Meanwhile, cut eggplants into 1cm slices; griddle-fry (or grill or barbecue) eggplant until browned both sides. Griddle-fry (or grill or barbecue) veal until browned both sides and almost cooked through.
Place veal on oven tray; top with sauce, eggplant and cheese; grill until cheese is melted and veal is cooked as desired.

On the table in 30 minutes

mediterranean lamb
with roast vegetables

1kg butterflied boned lamb shoulder

100g butter, softened

$1/2$ teaspoon finely grated lemon rind

2 tablespoons finely chopped fresh parsley

2 teaspoons finely chopped fresh thyme

2 cloves garlic, crushed

1 tablespoon olive oil

4 small brown onions (320g), quartered

2 medium zucchini (240g), quartered

2 medium baby eggplants (160g), quartered

1 medium red capsicum (200g), sliced thickly

4 medium potatoes (800g), quartered

Open lamb out flat; place, fat-side down on board. Using a meat mallet, pound lamb to even thickness. Combine butter, rind, parsley, thyme and garlic in small bowl; spread mixture over fat-side of lamb.

Heat oil in large heavy-based baking dish; cook lamb, uncovered, until browned both sides, remove from dish. Add onion, zucchini, eggplant, capsicum and potato; cook, stirring, until vegetables are browned lightly. Place lamb, fat-side up, on top of vegetables. Cook, uncovered, in moderately hot oven about 30 minutes or until lamb is cooked as desired.

Remove lamb from dish; cover with foil to keep warm. Drain and discard excess pan juices, return vegetables to oven; bake, uncovered, in very hot oven about 10 minutes or until browned.

On the table in 60 minutes

chicken

cacciatore

2 tablespoons olive oil

12 chicken thigh cutlets (1.9kg)

1 large brown onion (200g), sliced

2 cloves garlic, crushed

1 medium red capsicum (200g), sliced

2 x 400g cans tomatoes

1/2 cup (125ml) chicken stock

1/2 cup (125ml) dry white wine

1/4 cup (60ml) tomato paste

1 sprig fresh rosemary

1 bay leaf

1/2 cup (80g) black olives, seeded

Heat oil in large frying pan; cook chicken, in batches, until browned all over, drain on absorbent paper. Cook onion, garlic and capsicum in same pan, stirring, until onion is soft. Stir in undrained crushed tomatoes, stock, wine, paste, rosemary and bay leaf. Add chicken; simmer, covered, about 30 minutes or until chicken is cooked through. Add olives; simmer, uncovered, until sauce thickens; discard rosemary and bay leaf.

On the table in 50 minutes

tagliatelle with
smoked salmon

250g asparagus

200g sliced smoked salmon

50g butter

1 small leek (200g), sliced

1 clove garlic, crushed

2 tablespoons brandy

2 cups (500ml) cream

1 teaspoon tomato paste

$^1/_2$ teaspoon Tabasco sauce

1 tablespoon chopped fresh dill

500g tagliatelle pasta

1 tablespoon (20g) salmon roe

1 teaspoon drained capers

Cut asparagus into 3cm lengths. Boil, steam or microwave asparagus until tender; drain. Cut salmon into 2cm strips.

Heat butter in large frying pan; cook leek and garlic, stirring, until leek is soft. Add brandy, cook 1 minute. Stir in cream, paste and sauce; simmer, uncovered, about 5 minutes or until sauce thickens slightly. Add asparagus, salmon and dill.

Cook pasta in large saucepan of boiling water, uncovered, until just tender; drain. Serve sauce over pasta; top with salmon roe and capers.

On the table in 25 minutes

tomato basil
meatballs
with spaghetti

2 tablespoons olive oil

2 medium brown onions (300g), chopped finely

750g minced beef

1 cup (70g) stale breadcrumbs

2 tablespoons chopped fresh basil leaves

2 cloves garlic, crushed

1/4 cup (60ml) dry red wine

2 x 400g cans tomatoes

1/4 cup (60ml) tomato paste

500g spaghetti

Heat half the oil in large frying pan; cook half the onion, stirring, until onion is soft. Combine onion mixture, beef, breadcrumbs and half the basil in large bowl; mix well. Roll level tablespoons of mixture into balls. Heat remaining oil in same pan; cook meatballs, until browned all over, remove from pan.

Add remaining onion to same pan with garlic; cook, stirring, until onion is soft. Add wine, undrained crushed tomatoes and paste; simmer, uncovered, about 5 minutes or until thickened slightly. Return meatballs to pan with remaining basil; simmer, uncovered, until hot.

Cook pasta in large saucepan of boiling water, uncovered, until just tender; drain. Serve tomato sauce and meatballs over pasta.

On the table in 50 minutes

44 lamb and artichoke
kebabs

Soak bamboo skewers in water for about 1 hour to prevent them from scorching.

1kg diced lamb

2 x 400g cans artichoke hearts, drained, halved

1 large red capsicum (350g), chopped

300g button mushrooms, halved

garlic basil dressing

1/2 cup (125ml) red wine vinegar

1/4 cup (60ml) olive oil

1 tablespoon shredded fresh basil leaves

1 clove garlic, crushed

1 teaspoon sugar

1 teaspoon Dijon mustard

Thread lamb, artichoke hearts, capsicum and mushrooms onto 8 large skewers.

Griddle-fry (or grill or barbecue) kebabs until browned all over and cooked as desired. Serve with Garlic Basil Dressing.

Garlic Basil Dressing Combine all ingredients in jar; shake well.

On the table in 30 minutes

roasted tomatoes
with saucy basil noodles

12 medium egg
tomatoes (900g)

1 teaspoon salt

1 teaspoon cracked
black pepper

1 teaspoon sugar

2 cups firmly packed
fresh basil leaves

1 clove garlic,
quartered

1/4 cup (20g) coarsely
grated parmesan
cheese

1/3 cup (80ml) olive oil

1 tablespoon balsamic
vinegar

80g prosciutto, sliced
thinly

375g fresh egg
noodles

1/3 cup (50g) pine
nuts, toasted

Halve tomatoes; place
cut-side up, on wire
rack in baking dish.
Sprinkle with
combined salt, pepper
and sugar; bake,
uncovered, in
moderately hot oven
about 30 minutes or
until soft.

Blend or process
basil, garlic, cheese,
oil and vinegar until
almost pureed.

Grill prosciutto until
crisp, turning once
during cooking.

Meanwhile, cook
noodles in large pan
of boiling water,
uncovered, until just
tender; drain.

Gently toss basil
mixture in large bowl
with noodles; divide
among serving plates.
Top with tomato
halves and prosciutto;
sprinkle with toasted
pine nuts.

On the table in 40 minutes

46 chicken, mushroom and pea
risotto

1 cup fresh or frozen peas

1 litre (4 cups) chicken stock

2 cups (500ml) water

1 cup (250ml) dry white wine

1 tablespoon olive oil

300g button mushrooms, sliced

1 medium brown onion (150g), chopped

1 clove garlic, crushed

2 cups (400g) arborio rice

2 cups (300g) cooked shredded chicken

1/4 cup (20g) finely grated parmesan cheese

1/4 cup (30g) coarsely grated smoked cheese

Boil, steam or microwave peas until just tender; drain.

Bring stock, water and wine to boil in large saucepan; cover, keep hot.

Heat half the oil in a large frying pan; cook mushrooms, stirring, until soft, remove from pan.

Heat remaining oil in same pan; cook onion and garlic, stirring, until onion is soft.

Add rice; stir to coat in oil mixture. Stir in 1 cup of the stock mixture; cook, stirring, over low heat until liquid is absorbed. Continue adding stock mixture in 1-cup batches, stirring until absorbed after each addition. Total cooking time should be about 35 minutes or until rice is just tender. Stir in cooked peas, mushrooms, chicken and cheeses; stir until hot.

On the table in 50 minutes

pesto
beef salad

700g beef rump steak, sliced thinly

$^1/_3$ cup (90g) bottled basil pesto

1 clove garlic, crushed

1 tablespoon olive oil

1 medium red onion (170g), sliced

1 medium red capsicum (200g), sliced

1 medium green capsicum (200g), sliced

350g watercress, trimmed

250g cherry tomatoes, quartered

2 tablespoons bottled basil pesto, extra

2 tablespoons olive oil, extra

$^1/_4$ cup (60ml) lemon juice

1 teaspoon sugar

3 birdseye chillies, seeded, chopped finely

Combine beef with the pesto and garlic in a large bowl.

Heat oil in large frying pan; cook beef mixture and onion, in batches, stirring, until beef is well browned.

Cook capsicum in same pan, stirring, until tender; combine with beef mixture in large bowl.

Place watercress and tomato in same bowl; toss with combined extra pesto, extra oil, juice, sugar and chilli.

On the table in 30 minutes

spaghetti
bolognese

1 tablespoon olive oil

1 large brown onion (200g), chopped

2 cloves garlic, crushed

1kg minced beef

6 medium tomatoes (1.2kg), peeled, chopped

425g can tomato puree

1/3 cup (80ml) tomato paste

1 cup (250ml) beef stock

1/2 cup (125ml) dry red wine

1 teaspoon sugar

2 tablespoons chopped fresh basil leaves

2 tablespoons chopped fresh parsley

500g spaghetti

Heat oil in medium saucepan; cook onion and garlic, stirring, until onion is soft. Add beef; cook, stirring, until beef is well browned. Stir in tomato, puree, paste, stock, wine and sugar; simmer, uncovered, about 30 minutes or until mixture is thick. Stir in herbs.

Meanwhile, cook pasta in large saucepan of boiling water, uncovered, until just tender; drain. Serve bolognese sauce over pasta.

On the table in 40 minutes

potato, bacon and spinach

frittata

4 medium potatoes
(800g), peeled

1 tablespoon olive oil

1 medium brown onion
(150g), sliced thinly

4 bacon rashers,
chopped finely

8 large spinach leaves,
shredded finely

6 eggs

1/2 cup (125ml) milk

1/2 cup (60g) coarsely
grated cheddar cheese

Boil, steam or microwave
potato until just tender;
drain, slice thinly.

Heat half the oil in
medium frying pan; cook
onion and bacon,
stirring, until bacon is
crisp. Add spinach; stir
until just wilted. Remove
from pan.

In same pan, heat
remaining oil. Layer
potato in pan, sprinkling
each layer with some of
the bacon mixture.

Whisk eggs and milk in
large bowl. Pour egg
mixture into pan; cook,
tilting pan, over medium
heat until egg mixture is
almost set.

Sprinkle frittata with
cheese; place pan under
heated grill until cheese
is browned lightly.

On the table in 40 minutes

52 chickpea and rosemary
soup

2 tablespoons olive oil

8 spring onions, sliced

2 cloves garlic, crushed

2 tablespoons chopped fresh rosemary

400g can tomatoes

3 cups (750ml) beef stock

425g can chickpeas, rinsed, drained

Heat oil in medium saucepan; cook onion, garlic and rosemary, stirring, until onion is soft. **Stir** in undrained crushed tomatoes, bring to boil; simmer, uncovered, 5 minutes. Add stock and chickpeas; simmer, uncovered, about 5 minutes or until heated through.

On the table in 15 minutes

penne

boscaiola

375g penne pasta

1 tablespoon olive oil

1 large white onion
(200g), chopped finely

3 cloves garlic,
crushed

4 bacon rashers,
chopped finely

150g mushrooms,
chopped

300ml cream

*1/2 cup (40g) coarsely
grated parmesan
cheese*

Cook pasta in large saucepan of boiling water, uncovered, until just
tender; drain.
Meanwhile, heat oil in large frying pan; cook onion, garlic, bacon and
mushrooms, stirring, until onion is soft and browned lightly. Add cream to
pan; stir until combined. Gently toss pasta and cheese in pan with
mushroom cream sauce until heated through.

On the table in 25 minutes

54

chicken
tuscany

700g single chicken breast fillets, sliced thinly

$1/2$ teaspoon sweet paprika

$1/4$ cup (60ml) olive oil

2 medium brown onions (300g), sliced

3 cloves garlic, crushed

2 medium tomatoes (380g), seeded, sliced

1 tablespoon drained capers

2 tablespoons tomato paste

$1/4$ cup (60ml) dry white wine

$1/4$ cup (60ml) chicken stock

500g frozen broad beans, cooked, peeled

$1/4$ cup firmly packed fresh basil leaves

$1/3$ cup (90g) black olive paste

$1/3$ cup (25g) flaked parmesan cheese

Combine chicken and paprika in large bowl.
Heat 1 tablespoon of the oil in large frying
pan; cook chicken, onion and garlic, in
batches, stirring, until chicken is browned
and cooked through.
Heat remaining oil in same pan; cook tomato
and capers until tender. Return chicken to pan
with combined tomato paste, wine and stock;
cook, stirring, until sauce boils. Add broad
beans and basil to pan; cook, stirring, until hot.
Serve chicken mixture topped with olive
paste and cheese.

On the table in 40 minutes

with sun-dried tomato pesto

¹/₂ cup (75g) drained sun-dried tomatoes in oil

1 clove garlic, crushed

2 tablespoons finely chopped fresh basil leaves

1 teaspoon brown sugar

¹/₃ cup (80ml) olive oil

8 small veal cutlets (1kg)

Blend or process tomato, garlic, basil, sugar and ¹/₄ cup (60ml) of the oil until almost smooth. **Trim** fat from cutlets. Heat remaining oil in heavy-based baking dish; cook cutlets, in batches, until browned both sides. Spread sun-dried tomato mixture over cutlets; place on wire rack in same baking dish. Bake, uncovered, in hot oven about 15 minutes or until cooked as desired.

On the table in 30 minutes

mushroom and spinach
risotto

1.5 litres (6 cups) vegetable stock

1 cup (250ml) dry white wine

1/4 cup (60ml) olive oil

500g button mushrooms, sliced

1 large brown onion (200g), chopped finely

2 cloves garlic, crushed

2 cups (400g) calrose rice

1/2 cup (125ml) sour cream

250g baby spinach leaves

Bring stock and wine to boil in large saucepan; cover the pan, keep hot.

Heat 2 tablespoons of the oil in large frying pan; cook mushrooms, stirring, until browned lightly, remove from pan. Heat remaining oil in same pan; cook onion and garlic, stirring, until onion is soft. Add rice; stir to coat in oil mixture. Stir in 1 cup of the stock mixture; cook, stirring, over low heat until liquid is absorbed.

Continue adding stock mixture, in 1-cup batches, stirring, until absorbed after each addition. Total cooking time should be about 35 minutes or until rice is just tender.

Remove pan from heat, stir in cream, spinach and mushrooms.

On the table in 45 minutes

risotto milanese
with lamb

1 litre (4 cups) lamb or beef stock

1 cup (250ml) dry red wine

1 cup (250ml) water

1/3 cup (80ml) olive oil

500g lamb strips

3 cloves garlic, crushed

1 large white onion (200g), chopped finely

200g Swiss brown mushrooms, sliced thinly

1/2 teaspoon saffron threads

2 cups (400g) arborio rice

1/2 cup (60g) coarsely grated cheddar cheese

creamed mushroom sauce

20g butter

200g button mushrooms, sliced

1 1/2 tablespoons lemon juice

300ml cream

Bring stock, wine and water to boil in large saucepan; cover, keep hot.

Heat half the oil in medium frying pan; cook lamb, in batches, stirring, until browned all over and cooked through. Cover to keep warm.

Heat remaining oil in same pan; cook garlic, onion, mushrooms and saffron, stirring, until onion is soft. Add rice, stir to coat in oil mixture. Stir in 1 cup of the stock mixture; cook, stirring, over low heat until liquid is absorbed.

Continue adding stock mixture, in 1-cup batches, stirring, until absorbed after each addition. Total cooking time should be about 35 minutes or until rice is just tender. Gently stir in lamb and cheese; serve with Creamed Mushroom Sauce.

Creamed Mushroom Sauce

Heat butter in medium saucepan; cook mushrooms, stirring, until browned. Stir in juice and cream. Bring to boil; simmer, stirring, until sauce thickens slightly.

On the table in 60 minutes

glossary

bacon rashers also known as bacon slices.

beef minced also known as ground beef.

breadcrumbs

packaged: fine texture, crunchy, purchased white breadcrumbs.

stale: one-or two-day-old bread made into crumbs by grating, blending or processing.

broad beans also known as fava beans, they are available fresh, frozen and dried. Peeling the beans, though fiddly work, produces bright green beans with a subtle flavour.

butter use salted or unsalted ("sweet") butter; 125g is equal to 1 stick butter.

cabanossi a ready-to-eat sausage; also known as cabana.

cannellini beans small white beans also known as butter beans.

capers pickled buds of a Mediterranean shrub.

capsicum also known as bell pepper or, simply, pepper.

chicken mince finely ground fresh chicken.

chickpeas also called garbanzos.

clams we used a small ridge-shelled variety of this bivalve mollusc; also known as vongole.

cream

fresh (minimum fat content 35%): also known as pure cream and pouring cream; has no additives like commercially thickened cream.

light (minimum fat content 18%): also known as pure cream. Doesn't hold a shape but is pourable; good for use in sauces, soups and drinks.

sour (minimum fat content 35%): a thick, commercially-cultured soured cream good for dips, toppings and baked cheesecakes.

curly endive a salad leaf, also known as chicory.

eggplant also known as aubergine.

flour, white plain an all-purpose flour, made from wheat.

kumara Polynesian name of an orange-fleshed sweet potato often incorrectly called a yam.

lamb

butterflied leg: ask your butcher to butterfly a leg for you, or do it yourself, by cutting long the line of the bone, remove bone and flatten lamb open.

cutlet: small, tender rib chop.

French-trimmed cutlet: cutlet that has been trimmed of all fat by the butcher.

rack: row of cutlets.

strips: from the leg or loin, cut thinly across the grain into strips.

lebanese cucumber short, slender and thin-skinned; this varity is also known as the European or burpless cucumber.

milk we used full-cream homogenised milk unless otherwise specified.

mustard

seeded: also known as wholegrain. A French-style coarse-grain mustard made from crushed mustard seeds and Dijon-style French mustard.

Dijon: a hot, French mustard, creamy and full-flavoured.

oil

olive: mono-unsaturated; made from the pressing of tree-ripened olives. Especially good for everyday cooking and as an ingredient. Extra Light or Light describes the mild flavour, not the fat levels.

vegetable: any of a number of oils sourced from plants rather than animal fats.

onion

green: also known as scallion or (incorrectly) shallot; an immature onion picked before the bulb has formed, having a long, bright-green edible stalk.

red: also known as Spanish, red Spanish or Bermuda onion; a sweet-flavoured, large, purple-red onion.

spring: has crisp, narrow green-leafed top and a fairly large sweet white bulb.

pancetta an Italian salt-cured pork roll, usually cut from the belly; used, chopped, in cooked dishes to add flavours. Bacon can be substituted.

paprika ground dried red capsicum (bell pepper), available sweet or hot.

pastrami a highly seasoned cured and smoked beef, usually cut from the round; ready to eat when purchased.

pine nuts also known as pignoli; small, cream-coloured kernels obtained from the cones of different varieties of pine trees.

pizza base commercially packaged pre-cooked wheat flour round bases, sold in supermarkets in a variety of sizes.

prawns also known as shrimp.

pumpkin, butternut pear-shaped with golden skin and orange flesh.

radish a root vegetable with a mild to pungent flavour.

snow peas (also called mange tout("eat all").

sugar snap peas small pods, eaten whole.

rice

arborio: small, round grain rice well-suited to absorb a large amount of liquid; especially suitable for risottos.

calrose: a medium-grain rice that is extremely versatile; can substitute for short- or long-grain rices if necessary.

spinach the green vegetable often called spinach is correctly known as Swiss chard, silverbeet or seakale.

squash also known as

pattipan, scallopine or summer squash; small, flattish yellow or green-skinned squash.

stock 1 cup (250ml) stock is the equivalent of 1 cup (250ml) water plus 1 crumbled stock cube (or 1 teaspoon stock powder).

sugar we used coarse, granulated table sugar, also known as crystal sugar, unless otherwise specified.

brown: a soft, fine granulated sugar containing molasses which gives its characteristic colour.

swordfish steaks an oily fish, with firm flesh.

tomato

egg (fresh): also called plum or Roma, these are smallish, oval-shaped tomatoes.

pasta sauce, bottled: prepared sauce of crushed tomatoes and various spices and herbs, available from supermarkets.

paste: a concentrated tomato puree used to flavour soups, stews, sauces and casseroles.

puree: canned pureed tomatoes (not tomato paste). Use fresh, peeled, pureed tomatoes as a substitute.

sun-dried: (dehydrated tomatoes) we use sun-dried tomatoes packaged in oil, unless otherwise specified.

supreme: a canned product consisting of tomatoes, onions, celery, capsicum, cheese and various seasonings.

vinegar

balsamic: authentic only from the province of Modena, Italy; made from a regional wine of white Trebbiano grapes specially processed then aged in antique wooden casks to give the exquisite flavour.

brown malt: made from fermented malt and beech shavings.

red wine: based on fermented red wine.

white: made from spirit of cane sugar.

white wine: made from fermented white wine.

whitebait small, silver-coloured fish which are eaten whole. No gutting is required. Rinse thoroughly and drain well before using.

wine we use good-quality dry white and red wines in our recipes.

yogurt low fat, plain; we used yogurt with a fat content of less than 0.2%.

zucchini also known as courgette.

index

facts and figures 63

These conversions are approximate only, but the difference between an exact and the approximate conversion of various liquid and dry measures is minimal and will not affect your cooking results.

Note: NZ, Canada, USA and UK all use 15ml tablespoons. Australian tablespoons measure 20ml.

All cup and spoon measurements are level.

Measuring equipment

The difference between one country's measuring cups and another's is, at most, within a 2 or 3 teaspoon variance. (For the record, 1 Australian metric measuring cup holds approximately 250ml.) The most accurate way of measuring dry ingredients is to weigh them. For liquids, use a clear glass or plastic jug having metric markings.

How to measure

When using graduated measuring cups, shake dry ingredients loosely into the appropriate cup. Do not tap the cup on a bench or tightly pack the ingredients unless directed to do so. Level the top of measuring cups and measuring spoons with a knife. When measuring liquids, place a clear glass or plastic jug having metric markings on a flat surface to check accuracy at eye level.

Dry Measures

metric	imperial
15g	1/2oz
30g	1oz
60g	2oz
90g	3oz
125g	4oz (1/4lb)
155g	5oz
185g	6oz
220g	7oz
250g	8oz (1/2lb)
280g	9oz
315g	10oz
345g	11oz
375g	12oz (3/4lb)
410g	13oz
440g	14oz
470g	15oz
500g	16oz (1lb)
750g	24oz (1 1/2lb)
1kg	32oz (2lb)

We use large eggs having an average weight of 60g.

Liquid Measures

metric	imperial
30ml	1 fluid oz
60ml	2 fluid oz
100ml	3 fluid oz
125ml	4 fluid oz
150ml	5 fluid oz (1/4 pint/1 gill)
190ml	6 fluid oz
250ml (1cup)	8 fluid oz
300ml	10 fluid oz (1/2 pint)
500ml	16 fluid oz
600ml	20 fluid oz (1 pint)
1000ml (1litre)	1 3/4 pints

Helpful Measures

metric	imperial
3mm	1/8in
6mm	1/4in
1cm	1/2in
2cm	3/4in
2.5cm	1in
6cm	2 1/2in
8cm	3in
20cm	8in
23cm	9in
25cm	10in
30cm	12in (1ft)

Oven Temperatures

These oven temperatures are only a guide.
Always check the manufacturer's manual.

	C°(Celsius)	F°(Fahrenheit)	Gas Mark
Very slow	120	250	1
Slow	150	300	2
Moderately slow	160	325	3
Moderate	180 –190	350 – 375	4
Moderately hot	200 – 210	400 – 425	5
Hot	220 – 230	450 – 475	6
Very hot	240 – 250	500 – 525	7

Food editor Pamela Clark
Associate food editor Karen Hammial
Assistant food editor Kathy McGarry
Assistant recipe editor Elizabeth Hooper

HOME LIBRARY STAFF
Editor-in-chief Mary Coleman
Marketing manager Nicole Pizanis
Editor Susan Tomnay
Concept design Jackie Richards
Designer Jackie Richards
Group publisher Tim Trumper
Chief executive officer John Alexander

Produced by *The Australian Women's Weekly*
Home Library, Sydney.

Colour separations by
ACP Colour Graphics Pty Ltd, Sydney.
Printing by Dai Nippon, Korea

Published by ACP Publishing Pty Limited,
54 Park St, Sydney; GPO Box 4088, Sydney,
NSW 1028. Ph: (02) 9282 8618
Fax: (02) 9267 9438.

AWWHomeLib@publishing.acp.com.au

Australia Distributed by Network Distribution
Company, GPO Box 4088, Sydney, NSW 1028.
Ph: (02) 9282 8777 Fax: (02) 9264 3278.

United Kingdom Distributed by Australian
Consolidated Press (UK), Moulton Park
Business Centre, Red House Rd, Moulton Park,
Northampton, NN3 6AQ. Ph: (01604) 497 531
Fax: (01604) 497 533 Acpukltd@aol.com

Canada Distributed by Whitecap Books Ltd,
351 Lynn Ave, North Vancouver, BC, V7J 2C4,
Ph: (604) 980 9852.

New Zealand Distributed by Netlink Distribution
Company, 17B Hargreaves St, Level 5,
College Hill, Auckland 1, Ph: (9) 302 7616.

South Africa Distributed by PSD Promotions
(Pty) Ltd,PO Box 1175, Isando 1600, SA,
Ph: (011) 392 6065.
CNA Limited, Newsstand Division, PO Box
10799, Johannesburg 2000. Ph: (011) 491 7500.

Make it Tonight: Italian

Includes index.
ISBN I 86396 172 0.

1. Cookery. Italian. I Title: Australian Women's
Weekly. (Series: Australian Women's Weekly
make it tonight mini series).
641.5945

© ACP Publishing Pty Limited 2000
ACN 053 273 546

Cover: Potato, bacon and spinach frittata,
page 50
Stylist Jacqui Hing
Photographer Scott Cameron
Back cover: Tomato and bocconcini lamb stacks,
page 9

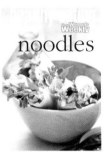